TONGUE TIED

WORDPLAY POETRY

Kendall Hope

INDIE EARTH
PUBLISHING

"Full of witty wordplay, sweet sentiments, and heartwarming humor, *Tongue Tied* is a nostalgic nod to the whimsical innocence of childhood and the riddles and rhymes that continue to shape and inspire minds. Kendall Hope's gem of a collection is the perfect read for the childlike heart of any age." – Amanda 'A.W.' Jones, Author of *Mosaics of Shadow and Light*

"Kendall Hope has done it again—a book of pure whimsy and joy! Her play on words causes us to pause and remember moments of elation, sadness, anger, and jubilation. This book of poetry is the older sister to every Shel Silverstein book ever written in that the idioms invite us to see a new perspective, one of imagination and childlike wonder. *Tongue Tied* is the perfect companion for any coffee date or day hike. Take a breath. Allow yourself to relax. And fall back in step with your inner child!" – Amy Harrison, Author of *healing: a collection of haiku*

"*Tongue Tied* allows you to reminisce on when times were simpler—like selling lemonade at the stand your parents helped build or the rhymes you shared with cousins on summer days—touching on love, emotions, innocence, child-like moments, and the less heavy times in life. For most adults, we fear growing up and losing the child inside of us, but with this book, you see that you don't lose that part of you if you embrace it." – J. A. Bishop, Author of *Her Colored Scars*

"*Tongue Tied* is delightfully unexpected, tickling memories of my earliest brushes with poetry. The pieces are almost off-kilter in the way they are steeped in joy, grief, and catharsis, even when the wording is simple and sometimes overly so. *Tongue Tied* sensed a gap that Shel Silverstein fans didn't even know they were missing… It's a comforting, familiar tea, spiked with just a smidge of something adult and cynical, signifying that we can go back, but only so far, and not without the faint stains of what we have come to know." – Jacquelynne Faith, Co-Creatix of the Sisterhood of Sacred Fire

"Kendall Hope brings a fresh vibrance through her words that will leave the reader elated and full of poetic wonder. *Tongue Tied* is a great addition to any library, leaving room to look at the world around us in a new light." – Fin Rose Aborizk, Author of *On the Ever-Lovely Morrow*

"This is a most enjoyable bundle of playful poetry. Hope gets to flex her considerable wit on a light and whimsical field. Like *The Princess Bride* or *Amelie*, it's something that simply makes me happy." - Ari Back, Author of *The Snail Factory*

Praise for *Tongue Tied*

"Once again, Hope blesses us with her artistry in more ways than one. *Tongue Tied* takes you back to a place in time where things felt simpler whilst still touching upon the depth of human emotions. You'll be reading these poems again and again." – Flor Ana, Author of *Amanita*

"Kendall Hope's newest collection, *Tongue Tied*, is a whimsical stride through fields of lollipops and chocolate dirt, with a stream made up of lemonade, freshly squeezed. It's like taking a ride on a kite through colorful clouds of spun sugar, with the wind occasionally whipping. This book is perfect for a sunny day when your body could use rest, but your mind wants to play." – John Queor, Author of *Bypass*

"In a world full of playful tongue, Hope walks us through fond stories, silly encounters, and observant wonders. Devouring the words of *Tongue Tied* filled my soul with laughter, adoration, and pure bliss. This is one of the best poetry books I've ever read." – Amelie Honeysuckle, Author of *To Kiss The Lips Of The Sugar Maple Tree*

"*Tongue Tied* radiates with joy, laughter, and sunlight. The poems explore the nuances of language, form, and imagery in a way that invite us to feel more deeply. This is a collection I see myself returning to, again and again, when I am in need of wonder." – Kristen Noelle Richards, Author of *The Desert Is A Woman Too*

"*Tongue Tied* draws on the whimsy of children's rhymes and stories, such as *Humpty Dumpty* and *Alice in Wonderland*, to artfully portray complex feelings of young adulthood. Love, stress, desire, and lamentation are expertly woven in, evoking a strong feeling of nostalgia, well-balanced with rhymes of lighthearted simplicity. *Tongue Tied* will resonate with any young adult, making them feel seen while immersing them in joy and melancholy." – Madeleine S. Cargile, Poet

"*Tongue Tied* is a poetic walk through the garden, with every bite-sized poem painting the delicate flowers with stories to tell and scents to leave behind. Celebrating a love for nature and highlighting the nature of love, this book is a warm, weighted blanket soothing the soul on a cold, blue day." – boy blue, Author of *METANOIA*

"An amazing collection of short and snappy poems. Hope's words are whimsical and witty, and I thoroughly enjoyed getting lost in each piece." – Jenna Stevens, Author of *Magic & Musings*

"A collection bursting at the seams with puns and play on words, Hope's work is equal parts silly and sincere and a joy to read from start to end."
– Heather Meatherall, Poet

Tongue Tied

Kendall Hope

*To the silliness and splendor
that go hand in hand in our lives!*

*"Listen to the mustn'ts, child.
Listen to the don'ts.
Listen to the shouldn'ts, the impossibles,
the won'ts. Listen to the never haves,
then listen close to me...
Anything can happen, child.
Anything can be."*

- Shel Silverstein

A Wonderful Play on Words
A Foreword by Flor Ana

Perhaps, like me, you grew up on poetry written by Dr. Seuss and Shel Silverstein; artists of words that have inspired my own works. Perhaps, like me, you have a deep love for puns and poetry that rhymes and brings you back to your childhood self and innoncence.

A wonderful poet as well as a wonderful friend, Kendall Hope and her junior poetry collection Tongue Tied have brought me back to a time when reading poetry is fun and silly—something we don't see enough of in today's literature—and I'm so excited for you to jump into this collection and ride along with the beautiful wordplay and illustrations Kendall has gifted us.

Once again, I am honored to have been asked to write the foreword for Kendall's work, and once again, I am blown away by the poetry that is the dichotomy of fun innoncence and melancholy depth. Tongue Tied is a collection of poems that not only pulls at your heartstrings but makes you recall rhymes and songs that perhaps had not crossed your mind in a long time. It takes you back to a place in time where things might've felt simpler whilst still touching upon the universal subjects of love, emotions and more that'll have you re-reading the poems again and again.

Once again, Kendall has blessed us with her artistry in more ways than one. Her illustrations have that zest to them, as they always do, and her take on things from our childhood bring a nostalgia that I haven't seen in a poetry collection in a long time.

If you take anything from this collection, in my own opinion, let it be this: you can have it both. You can be both young and old at heart. You can be both wise and innocent. You can be both happy and sad. And you can be both nostalgic for the past while looking forward to the future. Tongue Tied is able to bring forth such duality that I'm sure it will always have you discovering something new with each read.

Table of Contents

Table of Contents

Table of Contents

Table of Contents

Table of Contents

Table of Contents

Tongue Tied

Kendall Hope

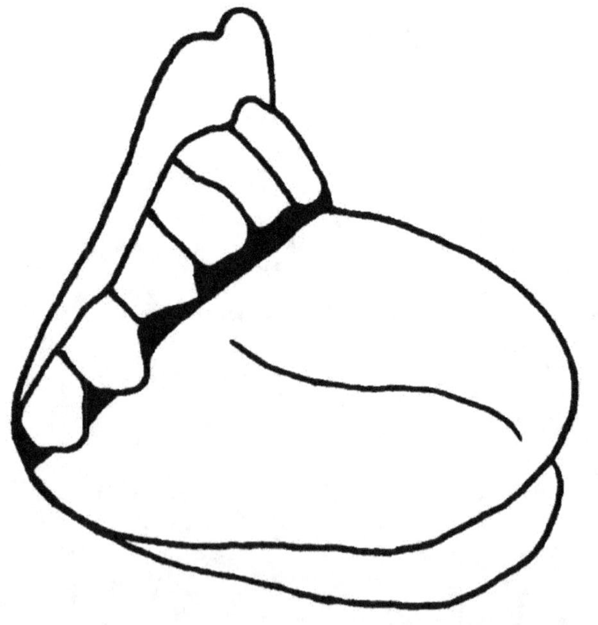

Tongued Tied

Hold your tongue
as quiet as a mouse.
Cat got your tongue,
let me help you out.

Leave me tongue-tied,
all I can do is rhyme.
Tie your tongue 'round mine.
Your words taste so divine.

La Lun(a Moth)

Sweet Luna moth
flies to the moon
each night,

placing dreams into
sleeping minds
as she flies out of sight.

Flowers' Morning Routine

As the bluebells of the garden
chime with the sunrise,
one can smell breakfast in the air
as the buttercups wait to be devoured.

The tiger lilies roar
to awaken the day.

Fresh as an oopsy daisy,
the morning glory's yawning petals
unfurl as she wakes
and dew drips from her chin.

Black-eyed Susan
stares at her neighboring florals
with pupils of admiration.

And I seem to be a wallflower—
an orchid mantis
trying to disguise myself—
as I watch the flowers' morning routine.

Acorn

A coincidence
A coincidenc
A coinciden
A coincide
A coincid
A coinci
A coinc
A coin
A coi
A co
Ac
A
Ac
Aco
Acor
Acorn

Honeymoon

Honey lover, honey butter,
honeymoon with me, my love,
and feel the satellite's sticky craters.

I(eye)rises

Iris in an art museum
framed beautifully.
The boy who likes irises
became one to me.

He said they smelled of cotton candy,
and his eyes are colored green.
I hope I may have found
my flower boy, indeed.

A garden blooms in my mind
and irises flood most of it.
Colors varying,
florals carrying
my dreamy thoughts of you.

All the irises were there before,
all along each summer, I am sure,
but I did not notice them
until you came.
So love, may I keep you
pressed inside a frame?

Bed Bugs

Sweet dreams,
sleep tight,
do not let the bed bugs bite.

Bugs bite
and your skin swells.
Oh dear,
keep the light on
and hope they do not near.

Little do you know,
they are snug
as a bug in a rug,
sheets tugged,
in the covers they are dug,
ready for slumber
and tucked in for the night.

Elderberry

I like to listen to the wisdom
that the old man's beard
and elderberries like to share.

Just listen to the woods
and feel their stories in the forest floor.

Grounded

Grow, grow, grow
but also remain grounded.
I remind myself to notice
where my feet stand right now.
I am planted
and this moment matters.

A puppy on my feet,
dirt below my knees,
color-changing polish
while there is grass between my toes.
River rocks under my skin,
and moments I can soak in.

Grounded.

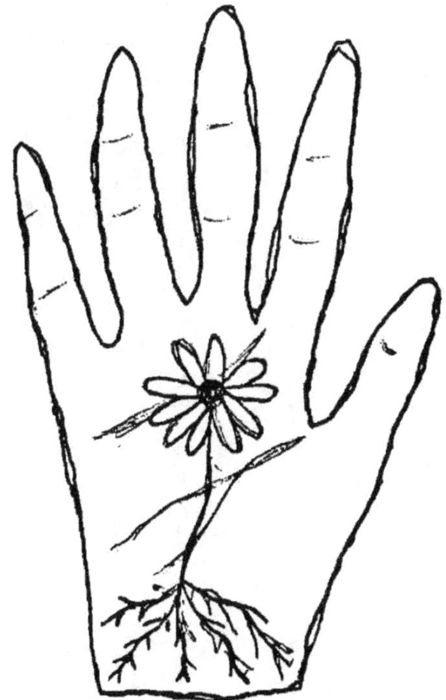

Among The Cosmos

Among the cosmos,
I lay in the flowers
and wonder of space
and meteor showers.

I stare at the sky
and feel the ground beneath me.
If the flowers were pansies instead,
would that make me a sissy?

Dragon Fruit

The forbidden fruit
held in the dragon's keep
flourishes on the vine.

Manage to find the root
and glimpse just a peak.
But pluck it from the nest
and it shall not taste as sweet.

Tree Hugger

I am a tree hugger.
The sweet girl.
The earth lover.

Thank you, dear earth,
for providing me with air
that runs through my hair.
For giving me the green
that tickles my feet.
For neighboring the sun
that gives my soul fun.
For running rivers
through my fingers.
For speaking to me
most kindly.

I cannot do the same things
as you do for me.
So, in return,
I shall just hug the trees.

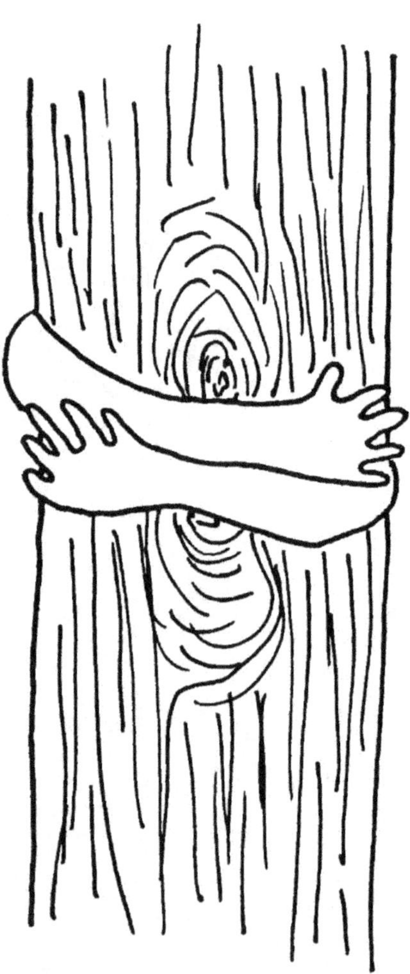

Unwelcome Mats

They say to make your brain
a nice place to live.
I do try,
but then, guests come to occupy,
passing through the
unwelcome mats of my mind,
ruining my space divine.

I am not allowing them to wreck my home,
yet they feel they can roam,
rummaging about my many thoughts.
They talk and they yell in my already
rambunctious space.
And though it can be wild,
it is mine.
And they are no longer welcome here
after this time.

Spiraling

Oh no Oh no Oh no Oh no Oh no Oh no Oh no Oh no Oh no Oh no Oh no Oh no Oh no Oh no no no no no no

Airport Purgatory

I feel the airport is like purgatory
and I am an earthling
stuck in a fever dream.

Strangers feel like ghosts
that pass me by.
And almost anything goes
as we pass the time.

Moon Jelly

Moon jellies and glow worms
dance among the twists and turns
of the spiraling Milky Way.

The space cowboy
rides his seahorse
over the sun's sting rays.

The cow jumps over the moon—
a moon made up of cheese—
with a man's smiling face
that controls the night's tidal waves.

And at midnight in the kitchen,
an alien craves
the jelly of a jellyfish
spread on toast
that comes from barnacle caves.

Strangers

Hey, stranger.
Still remember every part of my soul?
I remember yours.

Do you hear my heart
in the floorboard,
like Edgar once said,
thumping faintly for you,
in the back of your head?

Two Tin Cans and a String

We spoke so deeply,
and now it is as if
we communicate through
two tin cans and a string.

Can you even hear me?

Ella Vinn

Oh, little miss Ella Vinn,
she scores more than a ten.
With her blonde knotted hair,
playing in her childhood with no other care,
for miss Ella Vinn is only eleven years young.
This small ray of sunshine never feels high strung.
She sometimes has an attitude,
but she is not quite rude.
She has a light pink that sits on her cheek,
and she dances among the sparkles others seek.
Little miss Ella Vinn lives her days at eleven.
It is hard to believe she was not just seven.

Peachy with No Pits

A pit lies in my stomach
as I tell others I am,
"Peachy with no pits."

I swallowed a seed
and am building a mountain of fear
as I shed a tear
and sprouts grow from my eyes
and root in my belly.

Ebb & Flow

Caught in ebb & flow…

          My heart rowing to and fro…

My love stuck in your river,

        floating with no control.

Making wishes on the moon,

       she must have control over this too…

Do not want to wait for you

       & leave myself stranded,

but there seems to be no other

       so I wade in the waters.

Stuck in the

    e
     b
    b

         &

             f
           l
               o
            w.

Beetle Juice

Beetle juice sits in my cupboard
next to the juniper elixir
that calls for insect legs
and beetle shells
and is used in full moon rituals
and midnight spells.

In a Pickle

I called my mom on my banana phone
and told her I was in quite a pickle,
for I swallowed some watermelon seeds
and they are starting to tickle!

Toe Jam

Toe jam made of flowers.
I bury my feet in the dirt.
Scrape the gunk
and can it in jars
to later feed the earth.

Curiosity Killed the Cat

Curiosity killed the cat
& to that I say "scrat!"
Scratch of the match.

Candle dripping wax.
Wax left with the honey.
Honey so sweet, what a treat.
Treat others with kindness.

Your royal highness, the queen.
Queen bee whose honey is in your tea.
Tea on the table—oh, you spilled the salt.

Throw it over your shoulder.
It is bad luck.

As the black cat crosses your path,
does your curiosity kill it?

Anybody Home?

The lights are on,
but no one is home.
I am a firefly at your door,
needing to be lit by your love.

I am like a moth to a flame,
though the night's shade
is all I can find
on this doorstep.

The Blue Gill's Pet

The blue gill has a pet,
a blushing pink lung in a bowl.
Lovely little human,
in its small habitat,
simple as can be.
The blue gill and pink lung
dream of the sea,
sitting at the coffee table,
waiting for their tea.

Achilles' Heel

Bow-legged,
wrap me in ribbons.

Bruise my heart,
head over heels in love—
make me weak in the knees.

A phantom limb
once you leave.

Love me again—
you are my Achilles' heel.

Alrighty Aphrodite

"Alrighty, Aphrodite,
are you ready to go?"

he asks and does not mind the wait.

"Ready, Freddy!"
and oh, he loves her so.

Stupid Cupid

Stupid Cupid!
Where is my silly, little Valentine?
We were love birds
and your spell did not last.
It makes me wonder why,
but I have heard the angels
never leak reason or expiration date.

Mother of Pearl

I was once told
your emotions were as precious as a pearl.

So, I treated them as such,
kept them in the clutch
of my gentle palms.
Even when my hands grew clammy
from your worry,
I still held them tight.

I remember what you said that night,
telling me they were a pearl,
for, to open up
in a vulnerable ocean, is rare.
I became your swaying waters,
kept you safe & shiny.

Showing me your buried treasure
also made me feel discovered.

You are still as precious
as those sweet, pearly feelings.
Though today, I cannot keep reeling
for your attention
in the muddy depths of your sorrow.

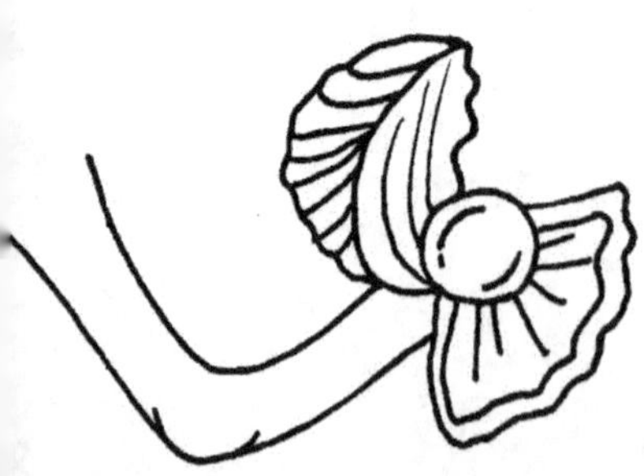

Blue Lips

Blue lips,
don't get your panties in a twist.
Do you miss my love letters,
signed, sealed, and delivered with a kiss?

Tulips ~ Two Lips

Oh, my lover.
Take me to the tulip fields
where our two pairs of lips
feel one another.
Oh, my lover.

Baby's Breath

Oh, that little baby's breath,
new and sweet.
Delicate and dried flower.
Nothing but mother's milk
that has touched the newborn taste.

Narcissus the Narcissist

Narcissus the narcissist,
flower of such grace.
Only full of one's self-bliss.
There is no bother to share your taste.

Oh, Willy Waily

Oh, willy waily,
you cry on the daily.
"Do not dilly dally
and act so willy nilly,"
wails the wilting day lily.

My Cup of Tea

I find you to be
my cup of tea.
Split a wishbone with me,
and hope I tickle your fancy.

For, you see,
you are the apple of my eye
and an absolute cutie pie.

Some would say as cute as a button,
but you bust mine
as my belly fills with laughter
and conversations over tea.

Honeysuckle

Suckle the breast
of the honeycomb
and may you flower with wisdom.

Do not mind the
judgment of others,
for it is none of their beeswax.

One Door Closes, Another Opens...

Door of blue,
a beautiful hue,
closes too.
I step outside
and start to cry,
hold myself and wonder why.

Step away,
the door has locked.
Not to see another day,
no matter how hard I have prayed.

Door of yellow,
sweet and mellow.
Comes close to me,
and out comes a fellow,
who meets my tired eyes
and shows me the sun again.
Full beams
stream into my soul—
they were there before—
but he brings so much more
light to my face.
And if that is the case,

please do not let this door shut.

Be the Bee

What is it like
to be the bee
that I watch
in this bush of purple and green?
To sneak in parts of the shade,
covered in leaves.
What would it look like in there,
if I were the bee,
and he were me?

Bell Flowers

The chimes of the bell flowers
cling & tink.
What do they sing
& what do you think?

Holey Ghost

The Holey Ghost
watches me in the corner.
He is a sheet
with holes in his crinkles
and he stares into the mirror
and says, "Holy smokes!"
Smoke and mirrors
reflect who he was.
A lover of the arts—
arts and witchcraft that is.
He misses his friends,
the murder of crows
that flew outside his window
creating shadows on his walls.
He creates shadow puppets
on walls that are now mine
and claims he feels,
"Finer than frog's hair,"
but I think that's a lie.

Brainwash

Perhaps my brain needs a wash
in a fancy clawfoot tub.

Maybe the hairs
on my shower tiles
are trying to tell me something.

Find a message in a bottle
that came from the drain
and figure out what floats your boat
to clean my brain of worry
and build my head a nicer home.

Ear Drum

My ear drum rumbles
as it follows the beat of my heart.

Conversation Hearts

Conversation hearts
speak without words.
Just the sound of two hearts talking,
through beats…

Thump, thump,

they go.

One says to the other,
"Why not be mine?"

And in response,
the other says,
"Maybe one day,
perhaps not this time."

Pink Gooseberry

"Oh, silly goose!"
I say as the goose on my porch
eats from the berry bush.
I do believe her name is Lucy
and she has gone all loosey-goosey.
Perhaps so have I
as it seems my brain
has gone south for the winter.

To Address the Elephant in the Room

I love you.

To Address the Elephant in the Room (Part 2)

Elephant in the room—
not visible to you—
but he is plump and overbearing,
crushing my mind.

I know, I know,
taking my time.
But man, this elephant in the room
is making me despise.

I want to care for him,
but I just force myself to not.
Ouch, ouch,
under his wrinkled bum.

I took care of him since he was young.
And now he squashes me,
no matter where I stand.

Cat Tails and Willow Wails

Cat tails
line the waters
on a summer evening stroll.

I can hear them meowing almost—
if it were not for the willow wails
that suffocate me whole.

Butterflies in my Tummy

All the happy little butterflies
you put in my stomach
flit about.
My heart flutters in admiration
as you slow dance
these butterflies out of me.

The World is Your Oyster

The world is your oyster,
but does it have a pearl?
Find it in the depths
of this sea we call life.

Tie it 'round your neck
and hold it tight.
The world is your oyster,
yet do not lose sight
of the rare and precious.

The Night's Nightingale

The night's nightingale
has a nightly tale to tell
of birds that crow
and oceans that flow
to help rest your head.

Can of Worms

Moths have no mouths
and unfortunately, I do.
A can of worms
spills as I speak,
and I feel like
a bug on a windshield,
but my words are not weak.

Chatterbox

Chatterbox,
I know this so,
I chat away
to the lazy bones.

They seem to listen
out of interest perhaps,
yet maybe they do not care
about my mouth that yaps.

Gutted

Absolutely gutted,
left with skin and bones.

> Ashes to ashes,
> dust to dust,
> dig my grave;
> I might combust.

Quicksand takes hold
and does not even begin
to scratch the surface.

> Stretch me thin,
> trace my skin,
> inside out,
> insides out,
> spilling,
> flooded,
> gutted.

Tipsy Toes

Tipsy toes,
just a sip,
under my nose,
cherry red lips.

"Sleep with the fishes,"
can no longer stand,
think up new wishes,
and float to dreamland.

Croak

Frog in my throat,
hope I don't croak.
Chirp with embarrassment
as I say the wrong thing.
Hide in the mud,
and let my skin soak.
Become one with the frogs,
I am already morphing.

Walking your Tightrope

Walking your tightrope,
I learned to fly.
I was full of so much hope,
yet, without any consideration,
you left me behind.

Tip-toeing around your love,
I grew my wings,
like a dove,
and found brighter skies.

Bottled Love

I bottle your love
and shelve it in colorful jars.
On my bookshelf,
I cork up the memories,
and when the light shines through just right,
I feel them all over again.

When Pigs Fly

It seems as though
I shall only receive
hogs and kisses
from someone in my dreams
and that it will only happen,
in person,
when pigs fly.

The Sound of a Tree Falling

If a tree falls in a forest,
will you hear it talk?
Struck by lightning,
left to rot?
Or just grow tired;
seasons fought?

Creepy Crawlies

Creepy crawlies,
fly on the wall.
The inchworm inches,
so very small.

The walking stick
hides in the twigs
and the ladybug lands,
bringing good luck.

The leaf bugs
want to be left alone,
and I spot all these creatures
on my walk home.

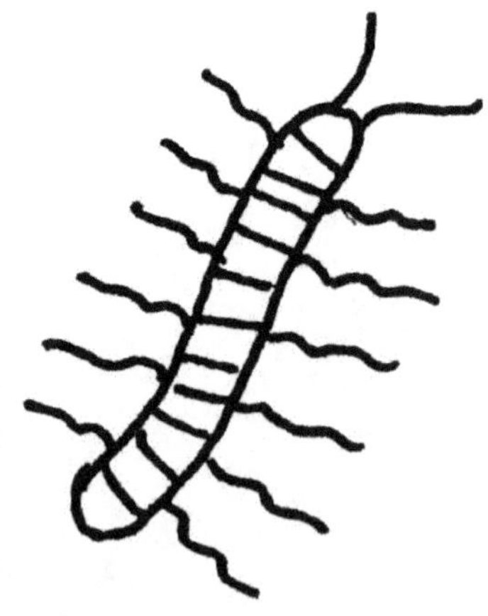

Spill your Guts

Spill your guts
to me.
Runny nose
until it bleeds.
I'll wipe your tears;
now brush your teeth.
Let's go to bed
and have sweet dreams.

Nectarine Neck Kisses

Nectarine kisses on my neck.
We eat and savor
this fruit of fragrance and flavor.
Our kisses so full of taste,
sitting here, there is no haste.
The juice drips off my hands all sticky.
I hate the stick, but love this.
The strings of fruit between my teeth
floss themselves until I need to floss myself.
Careful of the pit,
not to bite too deep.
Sealed with the kiss
of that sweet summer fruit bliss.

Dust Bunnies

Spring has sprung
and the dust bunnies
start to make me sneeze.
They want to be my pets,
but I cannot handle the allergies.

Snump

Snail on a stump.
He glides about his day,
basks in the sun
and knows it will
all be okay.

You'll be okay.

Crocodile Tears

Crocodile tears
as you look me in my eyes,
having wasted my years.

"See you later, alligator."

I knew it was a lie at the time.

"In a while, crocodile."

And you never became mine.

The Polliwog

Little tadpole
turns into a frog,
no longer a polliwog.

He ribbits and dippits his toes
in the bog
and leaps as sheep do
over the moon.

Turtles All The Way Down

It is turtles all the way down
and love all around.

Find infinite layers of it
as you look down
from the edges of the earth.

Walking on Eggshells

Walking on eggshells,
I would rather not tip-toe.
So, I shall stomp them so,
make paint from their powder
and create a new story.

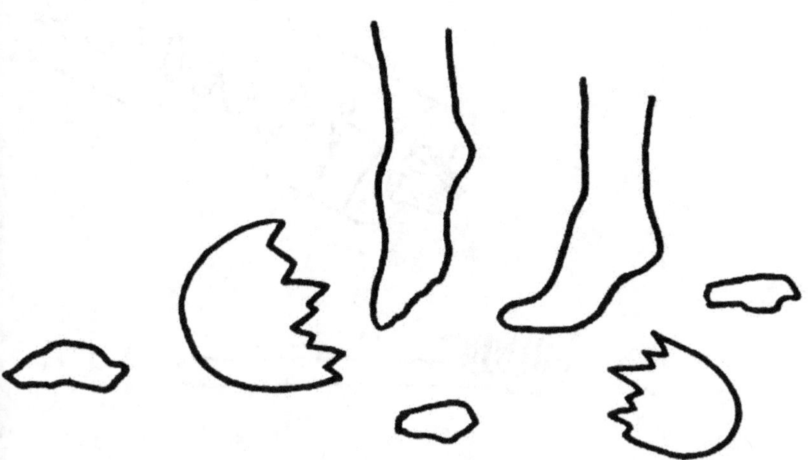

Toothpaste Kisses

Heart in your hand,
used to be another man.

String of thread
glowing red,
pulling not the slightest dread
between our heads.

Faces smiling
full of teeth,
never wanting
another man to meet.

May the tooth fairy
grant our dreams
of morning routines
and toothpaste kisses.

Early Bird Gets the Worm

The early bird
gets the worm,
though not always
on its own terms.

Fruit Bat

Orange, strawberry,
nectarine, lime.
The fruits of the bat
are rather divine.

Father Time and Mother Nature

Father Time tells me I must hurry
while Mother Nature soothes my worry.

Mother tells Father that he must allow me
my time to the ground beneath my feet.
He admires her and she finds it awfully sweet.

So, sometimes, he slows
and allows me to sit
while she helps me grow.

The Baby Girl

Let us wrap her up in butterflies
and dream her troubles away.
Sweet, little, baby girl,
growing out of her cocoon each day.

Grass Stains

Grass stains my jeans—
the ones that fit my legs just right—
as I roll down the hills of summer
and keep my inner child alive.

I dive into blades of emerald
and do not mind
that they make my arms itch,
for this is the life
I love to relive each year.

I swing upside down,
above the creek near my house,
and watch the sweet grass
grow from the sky
and wonder if it tastes
as sweet as it sounds.

And at the end of the day,
with grass stains on my knees,
I thank the summer
and the green on my pant seams.

Dandelions on my Birthday Cake

Make a wish,
you made it another year!
Let the wish-puffs
and candle smoke
manifest your dreams.

Fossil(eyes)ize

As a beast of the woods
roams through the night,
his eyes lurk through trees
and cause quite a fright.

Catch a glimpse of him
and notice the buzzing of flies
grows silent
and even wood becomes petrified.

Dance with the Devil

A wee devil
dances in my uterus.
He pokes and prods
with his tongs.
This devil's dance
I do not care to join.
My blood boiling,
I hope he leaves soon.

Gnat

The little gnat that does no harm
annoys me,
crawling on my arm.
Here & there, flying in a flash.
Little gnat, please leave my plants!

The Way the Mantis Prays

The mantis prays
over his prey.
Thankful for dinner
and to last another day.

Cry Over Spilled Milk

Do not cry over spilled milk,
I am told.
Time and time again,
my tears turn to silk
as they run down my cheeks.

And so I ignore
and let myself feel sore.
For today,
I shall cry over spilled milk.

Grief Counseling

On Tuesday mornings,
the black widow
& the mourning dove
attend grief counseling.
An unlikely pair,
you see,
however, they have worries too,
just like me.

Hippies That Say Howdy

I am to see the world
and grow with its lush
spaces of life.

To roam among the mountains
and hear the grass whisper
while I converse with strangers
and meet the hippies that say howdy
and are just like me.

Crayons in a Cigarette Box

"Have you got a light?"
the artist asks the other.

Exhausted with art block,
he finds inspiration in a smoke break.
Crayons in a cigarette box,
to rid his creative ache.

Gone Batty

Gone batty,
completely mad,
off the walls,
just a tad.

Headache

Thinking so much,
my head starts to ache.
I suppose it may be better
than loving so much,
my heart must break.

Sugar

Do the swallows themselves
swallow the delectable juice
of a peach during the fresh summertime
after a flight?
And do the sugar gliders taste
the sugar of the sweet
nectar air
on the same summer's night?

Sweet Tooth

The sweet tooth
speaks kind words to
his fellow female molars.

They know not to trust
him though,
for his cravings
are rather bipolar.

Sucker Punch

Sucker punch.
Harsh, never sweet.
A swift strike to the gut.
Candy hits my lips
as do my teeth.

Stomach in Knots

My stomach is in knots,
and, simultaneously,
a bottomless snake pit.
One where they bite at your ankles
and fog your vision
as you spiral
and fall deeper
into a confusion,
left alone in the dark,
with nothing but a sting,
and a stomach full of knots.

Knock on Wood

Knock on wood.
I wish I could
morph into the redwoods
and melt into the trees.

Turn into a seed,
root into the dirt,
and when I grow big and tall,
shed my many leaves.

Spoiled Milk

I thought we would defy the odds
and could beat an expiration date.

But you grew sour,
and no one wants to love a man
who spoils so easily.

Heart Sore

Mend my heart,
reap what you sow (sew).
Unrequited love,
this much I know.

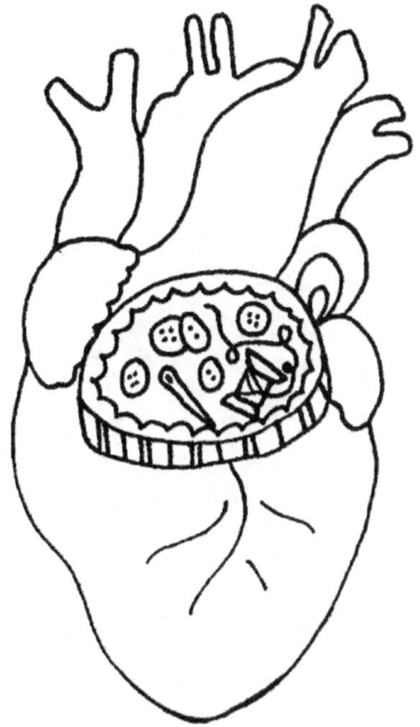

To Cry My Eyes Out

I cry my eyes out.
There they go…

Rolling across the floor,
dusty and cold.

Dandelions & Caterpillars

The dandy lion
guards the garden
with a brave heart
& good health.

The CATerpillar
munches among leaves
& lays about lazily
until it may turn
into a butterfly
& spread itself
on your homemade toast.

Humpty Dumpty

Humpty Dumpty
had a great fall—
as we all do.
And I cannot keep putting you
back together again.

Train of Thought

I was thinking today
of my train of thought
and all of the stops it makes
back and forth
and around the bends,

and that reminds me,

wait,
oh no,
nevermind…

I forgot.

Exhausted

Exhausted from the smell of exhaust.
Tired of being trapped in the gas.
Scent left on your clothes,
trapping the air with stench,
filling my lungs—
exhausted.

I'm Rubber, You're Glue

I am rubber
and you are glue.
Whatever you say
bounces off me and sticks to you.
Yet, I don't think that's true
because I still melted and wept,
and absorbed your silly, little words
and promises unkept.

Jinx

"Jinx!"
You owe me the pleasure
of being by your side
for the rest of my life.

Nine Lives

I wonder if we have past lives…
Nine, perhaps?
In this life, I find you the cat's pajamas…
Did I feel the same in our last?

Guarded Heart

Guarded heart,
wall of stone
with cracks for vines to grow.
Still open for the next suitor,
wanting to show my love,
melt me away
into oceans that reach
far past this stagnant moat.

Jack of All Trades

The Jack of all trades
practices many talents
in his house of cards
and masters none
at the end of each day.

Mister Plum

Mister Plum was odd and small
and had typewriters all over his walls.

Typewriters galore,
with lots on the floor.
Old, new, rare, blue,
and even autographed ones too.

A collection so neat
and owned by a man so sweet.
A memory so unique,
one I simply must keep.

Lazy Daisy

Lazy daisy
drives me crazy.
Shaking like a leaf,
oh, goodness grief!

Holly hock(s)
a loogie
while Rosy's cheeks
blush with disgust.

At least my sweet pea
is here,
keeping me safe
from the daffodils'
sneezing dust.

Mind Reader

Crystal ball:
I am a gypsy.
I feel as though
I can see into your soul,
however
I cannot read your mind.

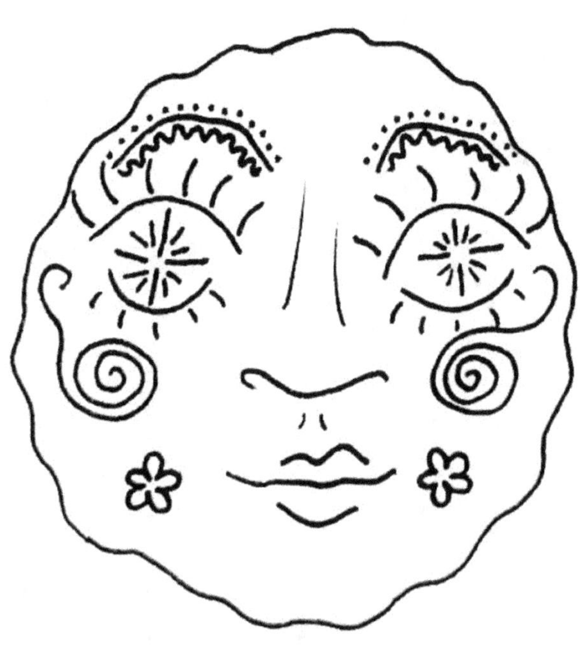

Knees Bruised Like A Peach

Let me garden
and play in the dirt
until my knees are bruised
like a peach
and tell me they hurt.

Love's Merry-Go-Round

I think love has harmed me
more than it has helped me lately.
If love is what makes the world go 'round
and I am full of so much,
why when I give and give,
do I not receive a single touch?

~

Silly girl,
as love goes 'round,
you shall find it everywhere
always.

Heart of Gold

Sometimes, the new becomes the old,
but its value is still worth its weight in gold.
At least in my heart,
or so I am told.

Mockingbirds

Warbles of the water birds
and mockings of the jays.
Spiders' silk and mothers' milk
seep out of nests and caves.

The bird's song stutters
in the wind that sputters
as wings flutter
and April turns to May.

Lying Through Your Teeth

Lying through your teeth,
words slip through the cracks.
Leaving me feeling weak,
my heart is under attack.

Mellow Yellow

I may feel mellow,
but he is so yellow!

His voice mellifluous,
the sweet yellow sings.

A rising sun,
he awakens my dreams.

Peek-A-Boo

Peek-a-boo
scare me true
when you start to peek
out of the blue.

Merricat the Merry Cat

Merricat the merry cat
was not so merry at all.
Her black coat
and yellow eyes
left a disguise,
crossed your path at night,
giving you the stereotypical fright.

Pigeon Coo(p)

Gideon the pigeon
sits in his pigeon coop
and coos to the crazy rooster
who crows at sunset
and shares the same roof.

Outgrown & Overgrown

Outgrown & overgrown,
vines consume my veins.
I dance along to my
tree ring record
and grow in my own space.

Strawberry Freckles

Strawberry-faced girl.
A kiss of natural pink
and freckles like seeds.
Pluck her right off the vine
and give her the love she needs.

The Hum of the Hummingbird

Here and there in a blink.
Flittering while its long beak
suckles the nectar from my hand,
where a flower rests,
between my pinky and ring finger.

hummmmm

Trinket Troll

Gifts are not my language of love,
typically,
but for thee,
I give you me,
in the trinkets you shall receive
that hold my heart
in an everlasting sea
of love,
for you.

Pepperoni Face

Pepperoni face,
garlic bulbs on show.
Everybody loves a pizza,
don't you know?

Shoe Fly

The lightning fly warns of thunder
to all the other bugs.
The shoo flies dance in puddles
in their wellies and their Uggs.

Off With Their Heads

"Off with their head!"
I say in my mind.

I shall join it for dinner
and eat my cake
across the table
as it stares at me
in disbelief
for standing up to their cruelty.

The Heart On My Sleeve

I wear my heart on my sleeve
and hear the birds and the bees
as I wait at the hanging tree
for love to approach me.

X-Ray Vision

Can you see
through my rib cage
how my heart beats for you,
beyond my words,
my touch,
and my gaze?
Cage made of ribs,
you must have x-ray vision.
Or else be blind
to not see why
I am so kind
to you, my lovely.

Paper Chain Dolls

I feel I am part of a paper chain
of beautiful female friendships.
So many lovely beings,
connected by souls.
I am never taking the goddesses for granted.

Starry-Eyed

Starry-eyed lover
looking at me
as I look away.
I can feel him,
moonstruck,
my universe.

Time Flies

Look at the clock and it shall tick slower.
The numbers melt
and tease me
while somehow,
when I am not looking,
time flies on the grandfather clock.

Hickory, dickory, dock.

Kendall Hope

Snake In My Boot

As I took a seat
in the saloon
and started to eat
my alphabet soup,
I felt a wriggle
and found a snake in my boot!

The Chicken Or The Egg

Who came first?
Chicken or egg?
Crack,
Splat,
Clack,
Chirp.
Leave me runny like a yolk.
Who even knows?

Wild Goose Chase

I have been on a
wild goose chase
this morning.
He was neither here nor there,
drove my head crazy,
so do not mind
the bird's nest in my hair.

Last One Is A Rotten Egg

They say the last one
is a rotten egg.
They also say
the best is saved for last.
So what is the problem
with having the fruit of life
and aging with grace?
To grow spoiled, wrinkly, and slow?
What a privilege
it is to grow old.

Notes

"Strangers" is inspired by Edgar Allen Poe's *The Tell-Tale Heart*

"The Blue Gill's Pet" is inspired by Animal Crossing

"Stupid Cupid" is inspired by *Bathroom Light* by Mt. Joy

"Toothpaste Kisses" is inspired by *Toothpaste Kisses*
by The Maccabees

"Off With Their Heads" is inspired by *Alice in Wonderland*

Acknowledgments

All of my thanks, once more, for my beautiful Flor. Flor is my mentor, editor, creator of Indie Earth Publishing, and close friend. She has grown with me as a person and in our creative world over the last few years. I consider knowing and working with her to be one of my greatest privileges. You inspire me deeply and I am thankful for you every day. Here is to what the future has in store for us.

Thank you to all of the many people I have met and loved in passing or deep connection. And here is to the ones I have yet to meet and love.

Thank you all for witnessing my being on this earth, as well as the words and art I have to share. My soul is fulfilled daily on this journey I have traveled so far and the days I have to come and look forward to.

My deepest and most heartfelt thanks to this life, the love it holds, and the connection it brings.

About The Author

Kendall Hope is a Colorado native, who thrives off of sunshine and creativity. She loves exploring the outdoors and being a part of nature, which translates into her poetry. In 2022, she debuted as an author with her poetry collection *Pockets of Lavender* and has gone on to continue her work with *The Willow Weepings*, which won a Gold Literary Titan Award in 2023. Kendall has also been featured in a variety of anthologies and her works can be found in local stores in Colorado Springs, like Poor Richard's, Ivywild School, and Barnes & Noble Briargate.

Visit Kendall on Instagram at @kendallhopepoetry

Author Photo by Hannah Benton ©
Instagram: @hanclicks

INDIE EARTH

PUBLISHING

About The Publisher

Indie Earth Publishing is an author-first, independent co-publishing company based in Miami, FL. A publisher for writers by a writer, Indie Earth offers the support and technical assistance of traditional publishing without asking writers and authors to compromise on their creative freedom. Each Indie Earth Author is part of an inspired and creative community, making a difference one book at a time. For more titles, or to inquire about publication, please visit:

www.indieearthbooks.com

For inquiries, please email:
indieearthpublishinghouse@gmail.com

Instagram: @indieearthbooks